Greater Than a Tourist - Hradec Kralove Czech Republic

50 Travel Tips from a Local

Tal Sheynkman

Tal Sheynkman

Order Information: To order this title please email lbrenenc@gmail.com or visit GreaterThanATourist.com. A bulk discount can be provided.

Cover Template Creator: Lisa Rusczyk Ed. D. using Canva.
Cover Creator: Lisa Rusczyk Ed. D.
Image: https://pixabay.com/en/hradec-kralove-homes-czech-republic-943678/

CZYK
PUBLISHING

Lock Haven, PA
All rights reserved.
ISBN: 9781549629433

>TOURIST

Tal Sheynkman

BOOK DESCRIPTION

Are you excited about planning your next trip?

Do you want to try something new?

Would you like some guidance from a local?

If you answered yes to any of these questions, then this Greater Than a Tourist book is for you. *Greater Than a Tourist - Hradec Králové Czech Republic* by Tal Sheynkman offers the inside scoop on Hradec Králové. Most travel books tell you how to sightsee. Although there's nothing wrong with that, as a part of the Greater Than a Tourist series, this book will give you tips from someone who lives at your next travel destination. In these pages, you'll discover local advice that will help you throughout your trip.

Travel like a local. Slow down and get to know the people and the culture of a place. By the time you finish this book, you will be eager and prepared to travel to your next destination.

Tal Sheynkman

TABLE OF CONTENTS

Tal Sheynkman

Our Story

Notes

DEDICATION

This book is dedicated to my friend, Filip Hruška, whose experience and advice were instrumental in the writing of this book.

Tal Sheynkman

ABOUT THE AUTHOR

Tal Sheynkman is a medical student who lives in Hradec Králové. He enjoys going out with his classmates to dinner in the beautiful Old Town, writing, drawing, cooking, and learning languages.

Tal loves to travel, has visited over a dozen countries, and been on trips exceeding two months. He enjoys experiencing the local culture by Couchsurfing with local hosts and trying out local cuisines.

"I am one of many foreign students studying in the medical faculties in Hradec Králové and have been living in the town for almost a year. I find this town particularly charming and hope to convey some of my experiences to future visitors to help them get the most out of their days in Hradec."

Tal Sheynkman

HOW TO USE THIS BOOK

The Greater Than a Tourist book series was written by someone who has lived in an area for over three months. The goal of this book is to help travelers either dream or experience different locations by providing opinions from a local. The author has made suggestions based on their own experiences. Please do your own research before traveling to the area in case the suggested places are unavailable.

Tal Sheynkman

FROM THE PUBLISHER

Traveling can be one of the most important parts of a person's life. The anticipation and memories that you have are some of the best. As a publisher of the Greater Than a Tourist book series, as well as the popular 50 Things to Know book series, we strive to help you learn about new places, spark your imagination, and inspire you. Wherever you are and whatever you do I wish you safe, fun, and inspiring travel.

Lisa Rusczyk Ed. D.

CZYK Publishing

Tal Sheynkman

WELCOME TO > TOURIST

Tal Sheynkman

INTRODUCTION

Hradec Králové is the eighth largest city in the Czech Republic with almost 100,000 residents, including a large student population. The name means "royal town" and, historically, the city was given to Bohemian queens as part of their dowry. Nowadays it is a lively, growing town with a young atmosphere, that remains largely unexplored by most tourists visiting the Czech Republic in favor of more famous towns like Karlovy Vary and Prague.

The aim of this book is to present Hradec Králové as a worthy alternative to the aforementioned. I would argue that for most travelers, the East Bohemia region, with Hradec Králové at its center, has plenty enough to offer to warrant spending their trip to the Czech Republic there.

I think Hradec is an excellent choice for travelers who want to take a step away from the hustle and bustle of the overpriced and overcrowded tourist traps in Prague, Kutná Hora and

Karlovy Vary. Hradec Králové is a town that does not see many tourists but still makes a noticeable effort to be hospitable to its visitors. A large body of foreign students means the locals are used to non-tourist foreigners and won't treat you as just another sightseer when you speak with them.

Here you have an opportunity to meet the Czechs in their own "back yard"; without huge crowds, pushy tour promoters, and inflated tourist prices getting in the way.

Almost every venue and event mentioned in this book is suitable for families, groups, or couples and prices range from free to exclusive, so whatever your means and the composition of your group, you will find something interesting and useful in these 50 tips about visiting Hradec Králové.

Tal Sheynkman

1. Arriving In Hradec Králové

Hradec Králové is located less than 90 minutes away from Prague by car. If you have the money for a rental car, this is the best way to get there. Plus, you can take a small detour along the way and check out Kutná Hora.

If you're looking to travel on a tighter budget, I recommend taking the train from the Prague central station. There is a train to Hradec every hour, but make sure you find out if it's a direct line or if you'll have to change trains somewhere. Either way, it takes about 1 hour and 40-50 minutes and you get a nice panoramic view of Prague, the countryside along the way, and a few little towns.

There are bus lines between Hradec Králové and Prague, of course. The price is about the same and the bus is 30 minutes faster, but the train is more comfortable and has toilets and a guy with a snack tray. Everyone I know in town usually takes the train, at any rate!

2. Getting Around

Hradec Králové is fairly compact, and all the interesting places are within comfortable walking distance from the Old Town and city center. Walking from the train station or from the central bus station across the city center to the Old Town takes about 20 minutes. The city has a good network of bus routes as well and a single ticket costs 25 CZK. All taxi rides within the city should cost 100 CZK.

If you intend to stay for a longer period and move around the city frequently, I recommend finding a visitor information bureau and asking about purchasing a city bus card. There are info bureaus at the Great Square, at the train station, and on Gočárova avenue.

To tour the countryside around the city, the easiest option is to rent a car. If you are physically fit and not in a rush, consider renting a bicycle – many places of interest are located only a few miles from Hradec, and there are many scenic cycling routes in the region.

Otherwise – most locations mentioned in this book are accessible by bus from Hradec Králové.

3. Use The Right Currency

Despite being a member of the European Union, the Czech Republic did not adopt the Euro and continues to use the Czech Koruna (CZK) as its currency. I recommend paying for everything with local money to avoid conversion charges. Many businesses might not accept foreign money at all. Local friends in the city advise not to exchange currency in Prague, and especially not at the airport due to the exorbitant rates. Tourist Infocenter is the safest place in Hradec Králové to exchange foreign currency and is located in the Futurum shopping mall.

As always while travelling, be aware of money scams and check the current exchange rate online before handing over your currency.

4. When To Visit

Deciding when to visit Hradec Králové is highly dependent on your activity preferences.

For sightseeing, I recommend visiting between May and September, since many sites offer their full range of activities and services only during the warm months.

For winter sports I recommend February, November, and December. You can get good skiing weather in January as well, but there is a higher risk of running into a storm.

By the way, I recommend having an umbrella with you even during the warmer months, as it rains fairly often and the occasional drizzle can still occur even in the summer.

5. Find An Affordable Place To Stay

I can recommend a hotel that I have personally visited in the Old Town.

Hotel U České Koruny is located on Tomková street right next to the Great Square in a renovated Medieval building. This hotel is an economy option with modest rooms, but is well kept and clean, and offers an affordable breakfast buffet. I have met the manager and he is a kind fellow who went out of his way to help me out when I first arrived in town.

If you are on a very tight budget, try one of the cheap pensions scattered throughout the town.

6. Looking For Extra Leg Room?

Adalbertinum Residence is located just off of Tomková street and offers very spacious, apartment-style rooms with regular room service and other amenities. Most of the guests are foreign medical students who stay there long-term, including some of my classmates. There is an adjacent restaurant called Tandoor - one of two Indian restaurants in the city - that offers a cheap all-you-can-eat lunch menu that is very popular with students and locals. I have eaten there more times than I can remember!

7. Start At The Great Square

The Great Square (Velké náměstí) is at the historic heart of Hradec Králové. Here you will find the finest examples of renovated Medieval buildings as well as an array of newer art-nouveau and cubist houses. The Great Square can be an excellent base from which to explore other features of the town, such as the parks, best restaurants, and walking paths.

8. Drink Plenty of Pivo

Everyone knows beer (or "pivo" in Czech) is cheaper than water in the Czech Republic. Perhaps that is why the Czechs drink more beer annually than the citizens of any other nation in the world.

In any case, Czech beer is considered by many to be some of the finest there is, and the best way to experience the local culture is with a mug of beer in hand.

Which beer to choose? That is a hard question. The four biggest brands - Kozel, Staropramen, Pilsner-Urquell and Radegast – are in fierce competition, and most bars and pubs in the city proudly declare their allegiance on their signs. Why not try them all? Let the cries of "ještě pivo, prosím!" ring out across the bars and pubs of Hradec, and enjoy!

9. Discover Kofola

I think Kofola is one of those things you either love or hate. If you are a fizzy drink connoisseur, you owe it to yourself to try this Czech competitor of Coca Cola and Pepsi. I can only describe the taste as something like a blend of cola and herbal iced tea. It's really unlike any other soda I've ever tasted.

Throw a bottle in your suitcase on the way home and bring it as a souvenir for your friends to try!

10. Satisfy Your Sweet Tooth

Trdelník may be a hard word to pronounce, but this unique and most famous Czech pastry, baked on a rolling spit in a special oven or on an open flame and often served with ice-cream or hot chocolate spread, is a definite must-try during your visit to the Czech Republic. If you've ever been to Prague you may have noticed that a dense network of dedicated Trdelník bakeries dominates the tourist hotspots. In Hradec Králové, Trdelník stalls usually pop up in various places in town around, and during, holidays and festivals - which makes them all the more special!

Another Czech favorite is called koláč (known in English as kolaches). These are small, round, puffy pastries with a dollop of fruit in the middle, that started out in Central Europe as traditional desserts served at weddings, and gradually became increasingly popular with the Czechs as an everyday sweet treat (even making their way to parts of North America).

"Don't go to the pub without money"

- Czech Proverb

Tal Sheynkman

11. Get Some Groceries

Not everyone has the budget or inclination to eat every meal at a fancy restaurant while on vacation. If you are intent on cooking your own food, you'll need to get yourself some ingredients.

You will find supermarkets such as TESCO and BILLA at the shopping malls. A mini-market chain called ERKO takes up the spaces in between the malls. Most of the healthy stores are concentrated in the streets around the Atrium mall, but the best-known chain of health stores in town is called Bazalka and operates a large branch on Gočárova avenue as well as a second, tiny branch in the Old Town.

If you are looking to chop up a fresh salad, the best grocers, with the freshest, juiciest fruits and veggies in the city, can be found on V Kopečku street.

If you are very serious about getting the full local experience, you can visit the small farmers' market outside

TESCO-Atrium (near the big, ugly, gray church – can't miss it). There you can get various produce items, herbs, and flowers.

12. Experience The Nightlife With The Czechs

Hradec Králové is surprisingly vibrant at night considering its population count. Parts of the Old Town can be positively crowded with people after working hours. Now is the time to really go out and meet the locals!

The night-club Nox, next to the Hotel Stadion, is the place to go for those looking for a party and a few good cocktails. Some of the best restaurants around the Old Town remain open until 11 pm or even midnight, and there's no shortage of bars and pubs throughout the city.

Have fun! And see if you can find out if the rumors about the promiscuity of Czech ladies are true…

13. Savor Czech Cuisine In The Old Town

The Czechs have developed a strong culinary tradition
that heavily features soups, thick sauces, sauerkraut and
knedlíky (a kind of dumpling), as well as several kinds of
dessert pastries that became popular throughout Central
Europe.

I can think of no better place in the city to experience the
rich Czech food than in one of the fine restaurants of the Old
Town. My personal favorite is Šatlava, a restaurant with a
fine-dining atmosphere located in the courtyard of a
renovated Medieval building with an interesting story of its
own (a prison?! Golly!), and a nice view of the Žižka
Gardens from the deck. The glass walls and ceiling over the
deck mean that even in the dead of winter, you can still enjoy
the "outdoors" dining experience and the view of the
gardens. Alongside inventive and truly delicious variations of
traditional Czech cuisine, the restaurant also serves one of the

29

best desserts I'd ever eaten – you have 3 tries to find out

which one it is. Šatlava is very popular but doesn't have that

much floor space, so reservations should be made in advance,

especially for evening meals.

Try the Svíčková sauce. Trust me.

14. Taste Foreign Flavors

If you are one of those people who really need a taste of home during a vacation, or just want to change things up a bit from the local food, a variety of restaurants in Hradec offer international cuisines for your dining pleasure. Most notable among these is Mexita, which offers a mixed selection of Italian and Mexican dishes and is part of one of the most successful restaurant chains in the Hradec Králové region. The restaurant is located in the Great Square and is open until the late evening. Mexita is very popular, especially with younger diners, but there are enough tables that a reservation should not be necessary.

For travelers with Asian tastes, the restaurants Noor and The Royal Maharaja, located in the Old Town, offer Middle Eastern and Indian cuisines, respectively, with a family-style atmosphere. Reservations recommended.

15. Go Skiing

Sněžka, at about 5260 feet, is the highest mountain in the Krkonoše range and in the entire Czech Republic, located north of Hradec Králové. If you are interested in enjoying some winter sports during your visit to Hradec, then this mountain, with its ski slopes, is the place to go. I have been assured by several of my friends who went skiing there that the experience was amazing.

You can reach the top of the mountain with a car, or via a cable car from the town of Pec pod Sněžkou.

During the summer, Sněžka and the surrounding area are also a popular destination for hikers and cyclists who come to enjoy the inspiring vistas of the Krkonoše mountains and the plains below.

16. Visit The Lions At The European Safari

Here is something you don't often see north of the Alps: an African safari, right on the Bohemian plains outside Hradec Králové! Zoo Dvůr Králové is a zoo and safari located in the small town of Dvůr Králové nad Labem (40 minutes from Hradec) that is open to visitors every day of the year (weather permitting). The zoo is an important contributor to international conservation and breeding programs of African animals and is home to a variety of everyone's favorite African species, including lions, rhinos, giraffes, and others.

Visitors can walk among the zoo cages or take a ride across the 178-acre safari.

You can even make a whole day out of it and stay at the adjacent Safari Hotel or Safari Camp.

17. Hike To Paradise

The Bohemian Paradise (Český Raj) Geopark is a 270 square mile nature reserve, the first and foremost in the Czech Republic. The name also applies to the whole area around the reserve. This vast and beautiful region includes sandstone cliffs, picturesque pine forests, and an array of charming fortresses and chateaus overlooking them all.

You can reach the Bohemian Paradise from Hradec Králové by car via route E442 (E35), which goes through the largest towns in the area of the reserve, or by public transport. You can find entry points into the Geopark's dense network of hiking or cycling paths at most any town or village in the region, but Jičín is considered the best place to start. Some paths are even navigable by skis during the winter. Other activities such as canoeing in the rivers, rock climbing, paragliding, and others are available at various locations in the reserve.

From personal experience, I heartily recommend consulting a local tour agency or visitors' center before jumping in. The Bohemian Paradise region is enormous and you could end up driving around for hours without finding any landmarks if you don't really know where you're going. Ask the folks at a nearby visitor's center to help you draw out a route through the area.

If you intend to explore the reserve on foot, I suggest planning to spend 2-3 days of active hiking there, to soak in all the sights. A much quicker way to observe the natural beauty of the Bohemian Paradise is to take the train from Jičín to Turnov, which passes by many of the landmarks of the region.

One of the key attractions of the area is the large number of castles scattered all over the place. I haven't visited them myself, but you could easily make a whole day trip just out of seeing them all.

18. Take In The View

The White Tower is the symbol of Hradec Králové and the most-easily recognizable landmark in the city. Looming above the Old Town, this medieval bell tower was renovated and rebuilt several times over the centuries and now performs as a tourist attraction alongside its usual bell-ringing duties. You can visit the tower every day, except on Sundays, and enjoy the interactive exhibition about the tower's history as you ascend up the stairwell to the observation deck.

From the deck you can look over the whole of Hradec Králové and the neighboring villages. The view really is wonderful; I know people who've visited the tower several times in one year.

If you are only passing through the city and have time to visit just one place, go to the White Tower.

Mind you, entrance is only allowed until 5pm.

19. Eat RAW

BistRAWveg is a raw vegan bistro located at Orlice Park shopping center, about 20 minutes on foot from the Old Town. Even if you are not a raw vegan, I recommend giving this place a try, as their food is very interesting! You can order a variety of main courses and desserts, such as tacos, "meat" balls, cakes, and more; all made without heating any of the ingredients to above 100 degrees Fahrenheit – thus conserving their full nutritional content. My favorite is the egg sandwich (with no eggs and no bread).

20. Meet The Elbe And Orlice For A Picnic

The Jirásek Gardens are the finest public park in Hradec Králové. Located on a triangular promontory formed by the confluence of the Elbe and Orlice rivers, this beautiful little park is teeming year-round with birds such as ducks and swans and, occasionally, other wild critters such as beavers.

Come enjoy a sunny picnic on the banks of the Elbe, throw a few breadcrumbs to the ducks, and try to make friends with a beaver. Perfect for families or couples.

"Down through the centuries, the Czech Republic,

the territory of the Czech Republic has been a place

of cultural exchange" – Pope Benedict XVI

Tal Sheynkman

21. Relax In The Hidden Gardens

If you, like me, are a person who would rather spend time with friends in a comfortable, intimate environment rather than at a bustling venue, or are just looking for a quiet and cheap place to grab some lunch, try one of the following cafes.

Bazalka U Dvorů is a vegan/vegetarian bistro café attached to a health food store with the same name on Gočárova avenue. The café is located in a charming and well-maintained garden on the inside of an apartment block, with the entrance facing K.H. Máchy street. The food is cheap, homely and wholesome. Be aware that since the entrance goes through an apartment building, the place closes quite early; so don't plan to go there for dinner.

U Lišaka is a specialty café on Tomkova street in the Old Town, with a menu based on crepes, sandwiches, and desserts. Delicious sweet or savory crepes for surprisingly low prices, and there is a back garden where you can enjoy some fresh air.

22. Engage In Fierce Battles

If you come to Hradec Králové with a large group, you may want to spend a few hours at the Firmsport Paintball center.

Located in the forest on the outskirts of town, this paintball center has a huge playing field filled with trees, realistic obstacles, and cover, including a trench and several bunkers which all allow for very tactical and interesting play. All playing equipment and instructions are provided on-site.

Coming here with my classmates, I've had some of the greatest Paintball matches ever!

23. Do Serious Shopping

If you come from a rich country, Hradec Králové could be a good place to do some shopping on the cheap side. Three shopping malls in the city – Atrium, Aupark, and Futurum – provide for all of your shopping needs with a mix of local and international brand stores. Atrium stores sell mostly British and Central European brands, while Futurum has more international suppliers. Aupark is newly-built and contains a few international brands and boutiques alongside small local businesses.

Each shopping mall contains a supermarket and a food court and all are within easy reach of the Old Town or city center.

A large commercial center is located on the outskirts of the town, as well.

24. Outmaneuver Solicitors And Beggars

In any decent-sized city, one is bound to run into a solicitor of some kind on the street at one point or another. If you want to avoid spending your time or coin on these people, you may want to know how to spot them at a distance.

First, surprisingly enough, are the Mormons. These Czech-speaking young Americans are part of a Christian charity that operates in Hradec, but they are not collecting donations. Instead, they are on the hunt for converts. If you have no interest in converting to Mormonism, be on the lookout for pairs of sharply dressed and exceedingly polite young lads prowling the vicinity of the Old Town and city center, usually armed with some book or a notepad. Even when it's raining, they'll be out there.

Second, beggars. You'll find them throughout the busy parts of the city. They are usually harmless and will leave you alone if you don't speak Czech, but I've been advised to stay away from beggars near the train station, as they can get fairly aggressive with demanding money from you. Keep your wits about you to avoid putting a damper on your vacation spirit!

Other solicitors can usually be found handing out leaflets outside the Atrium shopping mall or just wandering the area of the city center.

25. Walk Through The History Of Hradec

If you are staying in Hradec Králové and you decide one
day to go for a stroll around the neighborhood to stretch your
legs, I recommend following one of the set walking paths
that go through and around the Old Town and city center.
The municipality of Hradec established several walking
paths, complete with conspicuous info plaques explaining the
history of the surrounding buildings and the city. The paths
are all circular, so you can start your walk from whichever
info plaque you come across first.

The paths are an excellent way to quickly acquaint
yourself with the layout of the town.

26. Delve Into The Stories Of East Bohemia

The Museum of East Bohemia is one of Hradec Králové's most important and visible landmarks and a national Czech cultural monument. The building, with its allegorical decorations, was designed by the famous architect, Jan Kotěra, and houses archaeological, historical and natural science collections amounting to approximately 3 million exhibits, including highlights such as Queen Eliška Pomořanska's bejeweled belt and a large model of the city.

You can easily find the museum along the east bank of the Elbe; its blue dome is visible from many parts of the city.

27. Celebrate Queen Eliška

The festival of Queen Eliška of Hradec Králové occurs every year during the first week of September, to honor the Polish queen consort, Elizabeth Richeza, who ruled over Hradec Králové, which she received as part of her dowry from her marriage to the king of Bohemia. The celebrations include a medieval fair, street performances, a fireworks display, and much more.

The festival is a unique opportunity to discover Czech culture and history in a way that isn't available anywhere else. Don't miss it!

28. Remember the Battle of Hradec Králové

The Battle of Königgrätz (Hradec Králové) in 1866 was the largest and one of the most important battles of the 19th century in Europe. The armies of Prussia and Austria, totaling over half a million troops, clashed in the countryside between Hradec Králové and the village of Sadová, with repercussions that are felt to this very day (such as the existence of the modern nation-states of Austria and Germany).

Find out more about this turning point in European history by visiting the War of 1866 Museum in Chlum, a village near Hradec Králové. You can also visit the battleground itself, marked by a large memorial pillar. The area has several hiking and cycling routes that you can explore, strewn with more battle memorials.

Die-hard history enthusiasts, or even regular families looking for a memorable outing, may be interested in the annual re-enactment event of the Battle of Königgrätz, where

over 500 historical re-enactors play out a part of the battle

with authentic reconstructions of the uniforms and equipment

of the period and epic special effects and pyrotechnics.

Visitors are welcome to observe the re-enactment free of

charge.

29. Dine Like A Knight At Dĕtenice

The Medieval Tavern in the town of Dĕtenice is a grand way to finish off a day trip to the Bohemian Paradise area. This "Medieval" theme restaurant serves mostly meat-based dishes of traditional Czech cuisine while entertaining the patrons with belly-dancers, a fire show, and chaps in knights' armor running around amongst the tables. The service is rather rude but it seems that being sassed by a tavern wench is supposed to be part of the experience. You may also enjoy the live band playing Medieval music. This whole spectacle starts around 7 pm, lasts about 3 hours, and there is a separate entrance fee to the restaurant during the show.

The locals consider the food slightly overpriced, the locally-brewed beer excellent, and happily recommend coming to the Medieval Tavern for the fun experience and the adventure. You should make reservations ahead of time when coming to see the evening show.

51

30. Prepare For The Weather

Personally, I think the climate in the Czech Republic is perfect. The average temperature in the country during the summer is 65-70 degrees Fahrenheit. In the urban areas, it stays around 70-90 in the daytime and is comfortably cool after dark. In the winter the temperature ranges from 50 to 10 degrees Fahrenheit.

Once or twice per year, in January or February, it comes down as low as -5 degrees during the night in the lowlands, and even colder up on the mountains. I recommend not trying to go sightseeing in that kind of weather - even if you have nice warm coat on - because the roads become extremely slippery with ice and it's easy to fall and hurt yourself.

"If I were to arrive at a foreign country like the Czech Republic, I don't have to speak Czech to understand the feeling of the local sensations through architecture. That is the kind of communication that no language can perform." –

Jimenez Lai

Tal Sheynkman

31. Witness Fairytales Come To Life

Every September, the small historical town of Jičín, situated in the Bohemian Paradise, transforms into a Fairytale Town where local folklore and culture are presented to the public by actors, street performers, and festive decorations.

Every year the festival planners organize a variety of events and activities to entertain children and adults alike, including parades, tours on foot or by steam train, theatric performances, and much more. Visitors can meet Rumcajs, the Bandit of the Forest, and other characters from Czech folklore such as Manka, Cipísek, and the three-headed dragon; partake in various workshops; and enjoy the atmosphere of legends and folklore.

Even outside the festival week, the picturesque town of Jičín is a nice place to visit for its beautiful market square and the many walking trails in the area.

55

32. Chance Upon Mr. Masaryk

Named after Czechoslovakia's first president, Masaryk Square (Masarykovo Náměstí) is in a central location in Hradec Králové, somewhat removed from the traffic and noise of the main roads.

Various events and festivals take place there at different times throughout the year, and the square itself is surrounded by good cafes and stores. This calm, pedestrian-oriented open space in the heart of the city is a good place to go out for a meal or a leisurely stroll.

33. Connect With Your Spiritual Side

It's impossible to miss: the spires of the huge Cathedral of the Holy Spirit, smack in the middle of Hradec Králové's Old Town, are visible from almost anywhere in the city. This Gothic red-brick cathedral, the seat of the bishopric and diocese of Hradec Králové, was originally built in the 14th century, then destroyed and rebuilt several times during the turbulent 15th, 16th and 17th centuries, and was visited by the Pope in the 90's.

I don't think the cathedral is actively used for sermons and mass anymore, but it is usually freely open for visitors.

For contrast, you can go down to the square near TESCO-Atrium, not far from the train station, and check out Hradec Králové's newer, active church.

34. Take A Day Trip To The Rocks of Adršpach

The Adršpach-Teplice Rocks are a unique Czech natural landmark, located northeast of Hradec Králové. These sandstone cliffs were formed millions of years ago at the bottom of the ancient oceans, but now they rise high above the Bohemian landscape and attract thousands of visitors and rock climbers every year.

Follow the paths through the narrow canyons and over the tops of the cliffs above and find the giant stone turtle, the mayor and his wife, and other amusing and interesting rock formations. It's quite an amazing place.

To get the full experience, I recommend coming to the rocks with a local guide.

By the way, watch out if you are very claustrophobic. Some of the passages can get pretty tight!

35. Admire The Steamboats

The International Embankment of Lovers of Steam Engines is a unique event taking place in Hradec Králové every year in August; the only one of its kind in Central Europe.

During this event, visitors have the opportunity to observe and learn about various steam-powered vehicles and devices such as locomotives, cars, fire engines and many others.

Don't miss out on the genuine steamboats cruising along the Elbe!

36. Hear The Sounds Of Music

If you love music (and who doesn't?), you might want to plan your visit to coincide with one of the annual music festivals hosted by the city and the surrounding area.

Rock For People is the Czech Republic's largest alternative music event and attracts some of the biggest names in the genre, including Five Finger Death Punch, Massive Attack, Bullet For My Valentine and others.

Hip Hop Kemp is one of Europe's biggest hip hop festivals and occurs every summer at Věkoše Airport near Hradec Králové.

Finally, we have Jazz Goes to Town, an international autumn jazz festival that has been going strong for over two decades already. The performances occur over several days in concert halls, restaurants, hotels, and studios all over Hradec Králové, presenting to the public a variety of styles and a lineup of international and local jazz groups.

37. Watch The Games

If you enjoy soccer (football), you may be interested in watching a game at the Všesportovní stadium, where the local team, FC Hradec Králové, plays. FC HK was founded in 1905. Their greatest achievement is winning the championship of the Czechoslovak First League in the 1959/60 season. The stadium itself is pretty interesting because of its floodlights - they look like lollipops! The stadium can fit about 7000 spectators and is visited every year by many groundhopping freaks as well as local supporters. There are some plans to renovate the structure, but the unique floodlights might remain.

38. Drink With The Dragon

Don't worry, metalheads! Hradec Králové has something for your tastes as well. Batalion U Draku (Dragon Battalion) is a heavy metal-themed bar located in the Old Town, near the Great Square. Here you can acquaint yourself with the local metal scene and enjoy a few drinks while headbanging the night away.

39. Cool Off In The Water

Most of the hotels in Hradec Králové are not equipped with an on-site pool, unfortunately. If it's warm (or cold) and you are itching for a swim – try one of the local aqua parks.

The Flošna Swimming Pool is an outdoor pool complex with heated water, open only in the summer months. The complex contains several pools with water slides as well as a bowling alley, several sports courts, a restaurant, and more.

The City Spa – Aqua Park is an indoor complex, open throughout the year, with a spa center and a variety of water facilities such as water slides, a whirlpool bath, hydro-massage beds, and others.

Happy swimming!

40. Pay A Visit To The Countess

Častolovice Chateau is one of the most lavishly decorated palaces in the East Bohemian region, and possibly in the whole of the Czech Republic. This fascinating Renaissance palace belonged to the aristocratic Sternberg family since the 16th century. The current owner, Countess Diana Phipps Sternberg, who reclaimed her family's ancient holding after the collapse of the communist regime in the early 90's, extensively renovated Častolovice and opened it up to the public as a museum, art gallery, and park. A restaurant, children's playground, a small zoo, and a wildlife sanctuary were added later. If you are interested in art, architecture, and history, you definitely need to visit Častolovice Chateau.

You can enjoy the museum on your own or with a tour (which starts every hour), take a walk around the English-style park, pay a quick visit to the animals at the zoo... all in all, a great way to spend an afternoon, in my opinion.

Besides the famous palace, the small resort town of Častolovice, which is located about 20 minutes' drive from Hradec Králové and easily accessible by public transport, contains several other places of interest, including the Baroque church of St. Vitus and the late Gothic chapel of St. Mary Magdalene.

Tal Sheynkman

"Czech Republic's worst pickup line: what's a nice place like this doing around a woman like you?"

– Franz Wisner

Tal Sheynkman

41. Soar To The Skies In A Fighter Jet

If your pockets are well-padded with cash and you are looking for a once-in-a-lifetime experience, the team at Czech Flying Legends can definitely help you out.

Czech Flying Legends is an aerospace company working out of the Hradec Králové airport that offers demonstration flights on a genuine MIG-15 fighter jet.

If you've ever wondered what it's like to be a fighter pilot, this is your chance to find out for yourself. This isn't a simulation – you'll get to actually take off in this legendary Soviet jet with a trainer and perform acrobatic maneuvers in the skies above Hradec Králové!

What could possibly be a more unforgettable experience from your vacation in the Czech Republic than flying a real fighter jet? For those interested, Czech Flying Legends also offers a full flight training course with the MIG-15, complete with a MIG-15 pilot certificate.

42. Devour The Best Pizza Ever

Takeaway pizza is usually not something travelers look forward to on trips abroad (with the possible exception of visits to Italy), but I really feel I must include a mention of Pizza Pizza, Hradec Kralove's best pizzeria.

Their pizzas are quite literally addictive. The crust is sublime and they offer a selection of classic and original topping combinations. For a couple of weeks after discovering them, I was living almost entirely off of pizza...

They charge the highest prices for pizza in town with very good reason.

If you spend any length of time in Hradec Králové, I heartily recommend ordering from Pizza Pizza at least once. Delivery takes about an hour, depending on the time of day.

43. Go Back In Time

The Prehistoric Archaeopark in the town of Všestary, near Hradec Králové, is a venue rarely mentioned by tourist guides, but definitely worth a visit. In it, you can find an open-air museum containing full-scale reconstructions of Neolithic, Bronze Age, and Iron Age buildings and objects, where visitors can learn about everyday life and burial practices in Europe and other parts of the world in the era before written history – what their homes and tombs looked like, how they made their tools, what animals and crops they raised, etc.

At the Archaeopark, you will also find an exhibition building with three floors dedicated to themed exhibits about life in the prehistoric period – The Underworld, Life In Prehistory, and the Sky. Here you can discover the spiritual and earthly world of the ancients by examining the artifacts they left behind for us to find.

Perhaps the best (and most scenic) way to arrive at the Prehistoric Archaeopark is to rent a bicycle and follow the cycling path between Hradec Králové and Všestary, which leads directly into the Archaeopark and includes info panels with information about excavations of prehistoric sites in the region.

44. Explore Geological Wonders

It's a bit of a drive getting there, but the Macocha Abyss, a 450-foot deep gorge located not far from Brno, is the largest sinkhole of its kind in Central Europe and is popular with casual visitors as well as with pro cave explorers and divers.

The underground river Punkva flows through the Abyss on its way through the 18-mile long cave system of the same name.

Visitors to the Abyss can look down into its depths from one of two viewing platforms – Lower and Upper. From the Upper Platform visitors can catch a glimpse of the underground lake Horní, formed within the Abyss by the Punkva River.

If you're not planning on venturing out to Moravia, then the dolomite caves of Bozkov, in the foothills of the

Krkonoše mountains, may very well be the solution to all your underground exploration needs. This labyrinthine cave system contains several "halls" such as the Robber's Cave or the interestingly named Hell, decorated with beautiful and/or humorously shaped stalactite and stalagmite formations. In these caves, you will also find the largest underground lake in the Czech Republic. Just don't fall in the water – it's freezing cold!

The path through this one-of-a-kind cave system is not physically demanding and it's even possible to arrange a special tour if you come with a large group.

45. Be Dazzled By Precious Stones

If you like shiny things, the Bohemian Paradise Museum in Turnov is the place for you. This museum has displays about archaeology, folk culture, and history, but the star of the show is the geology and precious stones exhibition, which brings to the public the shiniest examples of the mineral wealth of the Bohemian Paradise.

Here, visitors can learn about the process of cutting gems and semi-precious stones, turnings them from raw minerals to the polished and lustrous forms we know and love from jewelry stores around the globe. There are also exhibits of famous jewels that belonged to important persons from history and examples of jewels made at international jewelers' symposia.

46. Admire The Jewel Of Czech Baroque Art

In the small village of Kuks, near the town of Trutnov, you can find the old Kuks Hospital – a magnificent Baroque spa palace built over the local mineral springs by Count Franz Anton von Sporck, and decorated with statues by the famous Baroque sculptor Matthias Braun. Once part of a much larger spa complex including a theater, a chateau, and other buildings, nowadays only the hospital, church and pharmacy buildings still stand.

At the Hospital, visitors can visit the pharmacy museum, the tomb of Count von Sporck, and a Baroque apothecary. Of course, lovers of art can appreciate the original statues of the Virtues and Vices by Matthias Braun, still found in the building. Outside the palace lies a park decorated with further works by Braun. Art aficionados rejoice!

47. Sneak Into Pardubice

Once you've seen everything Hradec Králové has to offer, you might want to sneak off and explore its neighbor and old rival, Pardubice – famous for its horse-rearing tradition and the gingerbread guild. (Just don't tell anyone in Hradec!)

The small city of Pardubice and the nearby villages also have an array of cultural monuments and venues worthy of your attention, such as the Pardubice Chateau, the Gingerbread House, and the Zelena Brana (Green Gate) Tower.

The Green Gate Tower, like the White Tower in Hradec Králové, has an observation deck open to the public, from which visitors can enjoy the scenic beauty of the Bohemian countryside with a view to the far away Krkonoše mountains and the nearby Kunětická Hora with the castle on its summit.

Kunětická Hora is a small mountain with a rich and

77

ancient history, a great view, and a castle that acts as a local museum and holds collections of archaeological and historical artifacts.

At the nearby village of Slatiňany, visitors can find the Hippological museum. Originally a chateau, the location now serves as a horse farm and a museum of Pardubice's horse-rearing tradition.

48. Learn Some Useful Phrases

Hradec Králové doesn't see as many tourists as Prague, and thus fewer people get the chance to polish their foreign language skills. You may find that most of the older generation in Hradec - those who grew up during the communist period - have trouble communicating effectively in English.

As ever when visiting a country where you don't speak the local language and the locals don't speak yours, it helps to memorize a few common words and phrases:

"Dobry den" *dob*-ree den – Good day, hello!

"Nashledanou" *nahs*-hled-ah-no – Goodbye!

"Promiňte" *pro*-meen teh – Sorry!

"Pardon" par-*don* – Excuse me…

"Prosím" pro-seem – Please, you are welcome!

"Jedno pivo, prosím!" *yed*-noh *pee*-voh pro-seem – One beer, please!

79

"Děkuju/Díky" *dyeh*-koo-yoo/*dee*-kee – Thank you!

"Co to stojí?" tso toh *sto*-yee – How much is it?

"Kde je…?" kdeh yeh – Where is [location]?

"Kolík je hodín?" *koh*-leek yeh ho-deen – What's the time?

"Pozor" *poh*-zor – Attention!, caution!

"Hlavní nádraží" *hlav*-nee *nahd*-rah-zhee – Central train station

49. How Long To Stay?

How long a vacation should you book when visiting Hradec? That depends on the focus of your trip. If you intend solely to explore the quaint municipality of Hradec Králové, I believe that two or three days should satisfy your interest in the town.

However, I would suggest that Hradec is better suited to act as a sort of base from which to go out and explore the East Bohemian countryside, with all its attractions and natural beauty. If you've already seen Prague and the other big tourist traps and still want to see more of the Czech Republic, a crossroads town such as Hradec Králové is an excellent place to start. Get a comfortable room at a nice hotel (or a cheap one) here, rent a car (or board a bus), and go out exploring to your heart's content. You'll easily find enough to see and do in East Bohemia to fill up your schedule for a week-long vacation, and more.

If you are interested in a more in-depth acquaintance with the places you visit, I recommend hiring a local guide from an agency such as Filip Hruška Travel s.r.o. (had a great experience with them. Reliable, knowledgeable, with a personal touch. Find them on Tomkova street, near the Partners Market building).

50. Moving On

So, you've seen Hradec Králové. You've climbed the White Tower, took a day trip to Adršpach, visited the East Bohemian Museum - the whole shebang. But you still have a few days left before your flight, so where to next?

If you've come to Hradec, you've probably already been to Prague, so why not leave Bohemia and visit the somewhat less-visited provinces of the Czech Republic: Moravia and Silesia? Cities like Brno, Ostrava, and Olomouc have their own stories to tell. I have heard that many people disappointed with the touristy Prague prefer vacationing in Brno, instead.

Perhaps you've had enough of the Czech Republic. Why not continue on to Wroclaw, a major city in southwestern Poland, or even to Kraków, Poland's medieval capital and best-preserved historical city?

Another option is Dresden. This German city is a

83

popular day-trip destination for both Czechs and tourists staying in the Bohemia region.

Protip: if you're heading back by train to the Prague airport, you can buy a ticket directly to the airport at the train station in Hradec Králové. It will be valid for both the train and the airport express shuttle from the Prague train station.

Tal Sheynkman

Top Reasons to Book This Trip

- **Nature**: The Bohemian countryside is beautiful.

- **Beer**: Some of the best in the world.

- **Culture**: A rich heritage stemming from the early Middle

  Ages.

Tal Sheynkman

> TOURIST

GREATER THAN A TOURIST

Visit GreaterThanATourist.com
http://GreaterThanATourist.com

Sign up for the Greater Than a Tourist Newsletter
http://eepurl.com/cxspyf

Follow us on Facebook:
https://www.facebook.com/GreaterThanATourist

Follow us on Pinterest:
http://pinterest.com/GreaterThanATourist

Follow us on Instagram:
http://Instagram.com/GreaterThanATourist

Tal Sheynkman

> TOURIST

GREATER THAN A TOURIST

Please leave your honest review of this book on Amazon and Goodreads. Thank you.

We appreciate your positive and negative feedback as we try to provide tourist guidance in their next trip from a local.

91

> TOURIST

GREATER THAN A TOURIST

Our Story

Traveling is a passion of the "Greater than a Tourist" series creator. Lisa studied abroad in college, and for their honeymoon Lisa and her husband toured Europe. During her travels to Malta, an older man tried to give her some advice based on his own experience living on the island since he was a young boy. She was not sure if she should talk to the stranger but was interested in his advice. When traveling to some places she was wary to talk to locals because she was afraid that they weren't being genuine. Through her travels, Lisa learned how much locals had to share with tourists. Lisa created the "Greater Than a Tourist" book series to help connect people with locals. A topic that locals are very passionate about sharing.

> TOURIST

GREATER THAN A TOURIST

Notes

Made in the USA
Las Vegas, NV
17 December 2021